I Wrote This

Shreya & Craig

First published in 2019 by

Becomeshakespeare.com

Wordit Content Design & Editing Services Pvt Ltd
Unit - 26, Building A -1, Nr Wadala RTO,
Wadala (East), Mumbai 400037, India
T: +91 8080226699
Wordit Art Fund helps deserving authors publish their work by providing monetary support. To apply for funding, please visit us at www.BecomeShakespeare.com

Copyrights © Shreya Sethi and Craig Dominic Pinto, 2019

All rights reserved. Any unauthorized reprint or use of this material is prohibited. No part of this book may be reproduced or transmitted in any form or by any means, electronic or mechanical, including photocopying, recording, or by any information storage and retrieval system without express written permission from the author/publisher.

Please do not participate in or encourage piracy of copyrighted materials in violation of the author's rights. Purchase only authorized editions.

©

ISBN - 978-93-88930-65-9

To Mom & Dad

Acknowledgements

If only we could whisper a 'thank you' that would echo forever into the ears of all those we are grateful to:

Our parents and family, who have always encouraged us to play with words and defy our boundaries; our ever supportive family of friends specially, whose contributions can't be calculated; Annika Bhasker, Udit Bhasker and Dhruv Randhawa, for designing and conceptualizing our cover and back page.

The team at *BecomeShakespeare,* who have truly lived up to their promise and given us the Word It Art Fund scholarship as way to encourage us to keep writing; Ragini Letitia Singh and Shantanu Thada; our editors, who showed us our true potential; and our college classmates who always celebrated our poems in good spirit.

Introduction

I bring to you a story of two very different writers, with equally varied styles of penmanship, from very different backgrounds; on a united journey. By the power invested in them by me, I present a tale by two poetic rivals or perhaps two poetic lovers; on a voyage into a world created by them. It begins where it all began and it ends at point from where they now seek 'a new beginning'. The words that dripped from their pens flowed straight from their hearts. Some written with good memories, some with bad and it was only paper, their loyal companion that stood by to capture their every tiny emotion. I wrote this, and they are like my two hands; clapping together in perfect harmony.

Preface

People unknowingly experience a lot, yet very few them cherished their experiences with the passage of time. When an idea brings two people together, there exists a purpose. During the discovery of one such moment, a friendship bloomed and bore fruit.

The purpose was to tell a single story, uniting the experiences of two writers who came together as one.

Our journey began 6 years ago, when the seed of an idea was planted. Once at a casual meeting, reading through each other's pieces made us realise, we were clearly heading in the same direction. The roots of trust finally found fertile ground.

The meetings multiplied with time, the friendship matured and the leaves turned into pages. Such was our journey, and we urge you not to distinguish our paths, but to travel with us through our experiences, one by one; to fully understand our purpose.

The once dormant seeds have now grown fruit, ready for harvest. With the succulent bounty of our passion and the endless branches of hope extending toward the sky; we knew there was no looking back, now that the ground was left far behind.

Contents

1. Created For Creation — 13
2. God's Wife — 15
3. Then Came Man — 17
4. Whoa! - man — 19
5. What God Did On The Seventh — 22
6. Perfect 10 — 23
7. Eternal — 24
8. Distance From The Sun — 25
9. That Night — 27
10. Thorn With Petals — 29
11. What Shines For Me — 30
12. Not Thinking Of You — 31
13. What Nature Can't Provide — 32
14. Just As Nature Ever Thought — 34
15. Love You till the End (Story) — 35
16. Climbing A Ladder — 42
17. The Last Petal — 43
18. Hollow Promises — 44
19. Linger On — 45
20. Imagine You There — 46
21. Flames — 47
22. Forsaken — 48

23. Silent Sword	49
24. A Phase	51
25. Pain	53
26. The Mask I Wore	54
27. Forbidden Fruit	55
28. Betrayal	56
29. Notorious Candle	58
30. Quest for Lust	60
31. Last Letter	62
32. Despair In Death Too	64
33. Last Nail Into The Coffin	65
34. Dream	66
35. Melting Desires	67
36. Dragon And The Butterfly	68
37. Uncanny Connections	69
38. I Didn't Know	70
39. Blind Sight	71
40. Destined (Story)	73
41. Dare To Dream	79
42. Behind The Scene	80
43. I Can Sir	81
44. Show Mercy	83
45. Tree Of Zorn	85
46. Singes Of The Sun	86

47. Whispers Of The Wind	88
48. Nature's Finale	90
49. Doom Monsoon	92
50. Her Words	93
51. Despicable Vows (Story)	94
52. My Birth Was Not A Sin	98
53. Maiden	101
54. Beggar's Question	102
55. Rural Misery	103
56. Rooftops, Lanes and Spirits (Story)	105
57. From Above I See	110
58. True Hues	112
59. Seats	113
60. I Wished	115
61. Metro Mania	117
62. Loading…	119
63. Addiction	120
64. Fake Reality	121
65. Hillness	122
66. Black and White Autumn	124
67. A Drop Of Dew	126
68. A Night I Remember (Story)	127
69. Playful Times	131
70. Lunch Box	132

71. Eternal Hope	135
72. From Wick And Wax	136
73. Learn	137
74. Lake	138
75. Leap	140
76. Beam	141
77. Light Of The Future	142
78. Last Night's Dream	144
79. Destiny	145
80. Why I Can't Write	146

Created For Creation

We're all made for a purpose
Like a match stick produces a flame
But some choose to keep burning
To burn forever is their aim

Every morning we wake up
The light of truth hits our eyes
We try to burn slower and dimmer
But the darkness can't mute our cries

The cries of monotonous silence
Which reverberate in our mind
The hunger for creation
Devours pestilent particles of any kind

Did God choose to rest
Until his masterpiece was complete?
Does an artist beat his chest
Until his satisfaction is replete?

For too long has my flame thirsted
For the spirit of inflammable fame
It burns long enough for you to thirst
For its sweet splendor again

And again and again
I will burn bigger and brighter
Tormented by the wind
I'll fight to face my fighter

I'll rise out of the cold
I'll learn to cheat death
In the absence of air
I'll learn to hold my breath

Until I fulfill my purpose
I'll burn hot enough to melt lead
Illuminating the darkness for others
Incinerating the cries in my head

We can't deny our existence
No dearth dares plague our door
An artist goes on burning
Until his flame burns no more

God's Wife

In the beginning
Before there came light
The creator and his preserver
Got into a legendary fight

Women came from Adam
That's what the world was led to believe
But it was his loving mother
Who decided her child needed the love of Eve

So God and his wife
Suddenly started fighting
He brought down the thunder
She got out the lightning

His wrath rose hills and mountains
Her tears filled the oceans and seas
God then made inverted fountains
Called waterfalls, so that she would cease

But who won the battle?
Any inquisitive mortal would ask
No one, they're still probably fighting
Trying to be the one standing last

That's why men vex their wives
And wives play games with their hearts
Deciding to combine two lives
Is when the trouble starts

So even today
The reason is unclear
The love-hate battle
Will never end, I fear

Then Came Man

When I first opened my eyes
I got a glimpse of a perfect world
There were so many wonders apart from me
As the cosmos celestially unfurled

With climate and geographic change
I saw, how many couldn't survive
Though it felt like I was losing something
It taught me how to cherish life

Then it was fore told
The greatest beast would rise
From the sand of earth
And the breath of sky

It would enslave me
And become my master
It would bring chaos and death
Bringing Armageddon faster

But I along with the others
Were told to stay silent
Knowing everything around
We tried to dissolve the violent

We tried to appease it
And some arrogantly displeased it
They were then hunted and captured
Every kind of mammal, fish and bird

We feared its footsteps, the day
It was thrown out of paradise
And every breath he took
Echoed with innocent's cries

Whoa! - Man

All alone in Eden
Adam prayed to God
Please do something, I'm lonely
So God gave Adam a nod

What do you desire?
Something that sets my heart on fire

Shall I give you a mate?
Oh! yes God at any given rate
But I will require a finger
Heavenly father! how can that thought linger?

I will take a toe
Oh! no God, anything but that I know
Fine, I shall take a rib
Father I have plenty, I won't crib

Son I must warn you
She is complicated and smart
Don't worry father
I was there from the start

She can manipulate and use you
Captivate and seduce you
I can impress and love her
Intimidate and shove her

You will have to maintain and move her heart
I will use my charm like an infectious Cupid's dart
She will empower you and make you an addict
No Father, I promise to be firm and strict

My child can I give you something else instead?
No dear God, you have instilled her in my head
First you must sleep, so that a rib I may take
Feel free dear God, I know exactly what's at stake

Are you sure my child?
She will take up all you time
I promise to spend time with both of you
If that's no crime

Adam I will ask you this once more
Is this exactly what you wish for? [Here comes the fall of Man]

The bull has his cow
The dog has his bitch
I know she will be something like them
But I'm not sure which

I grant you this wish for I love you so dearly my son
Sleep now, and wake up to the most beautiful creature under the sun
Adam rubbed his eyes and watched as she slowly woke
He carefully approached her and gave her a poke

It suddenly began to rain and thunder
And Eve began to shout and yell
Adam you're a blunder, I'm so cold and so hungry
I can't even tell?

Adam returned with raw meat
And lamb skin which had bad smell
The fury he faced that night convinced Adam
His life now was a living hell

The next morning Eve said "Adam your mine forever,
As a gift I want a diamond mine"
Yes dearest you shall have it all
{Dear God what a heavy fine}

The next moment Adam prayed to God
Why didn't you warn me enough?
Forgive me for I know I crib
My son you got exactly what you asked for
Because you only gave a rib

What God Did On The Seventh

If ever you see her
Expect your troubles to inexplicably fade
Her immaculate radiance
Makes you want to serenade
Entrapping all those
Who take their glance
In an unending mysterious
Bedazzled trance
I'm sure there are other victims
Of her 'have a nice day' smile
Her exceptional mundane elegance
Which makes time so worthwhile
No man can ignore her advances
Its beyond the power of human will
A benevolent creature like her
Could urge a saint to better himself still
Be careful not to look
Straight into those gorgeous eyes
Who knows at what level
This devil is an angel in disguise
To this perfect imperfection
Only a certain compliment holds true
If God took six days to create the world
He took the seventh off to create you

Perfect 10

Things couldn't get any worse
Good times looked so historically far
And the better times were the curse
I often questioned 'who you are'
You gave me hope
And I gave myself time
To heal and cope
From the punishment of my crime
Did I deserve this, or was it fate
That fortune would smile
Upon my face so late
Later than never
I thankfully pray
You came into my life
10 months today
10 months sooner
I may not have seen
A fatal reality
For I was a teen
10 months later
I just cannot believe
Things can get any better
I'd be a fool to ever leave
And now in 60 days
A Year, I'll proudly say then
10 months of imperfection pays
A 100%, to be with a 10

Eternal

Sands of time don't wait for us
We fly with the wind
Every time we meet
Time stands still
Mirrors reflect an illusion
You reflect me
No masks, no cloaks
To hide who we are
Yet, in the galaxy
We are just two shiny stars
We wiped each other's tears
And held hands in times of fears
What more do I need to say
Of the times we spent together
Eternity is not till we last
Each moment with you is eternal

Distance From The Sun

In the beginning my journey was short
Arriving at my destination on time
Feeling a sense of fulfillment
As the sun would send me sunshine

Every step I took towards the horizon
Taught me experience is gold
Sometimes love
Or just a kiss goodbye
Something always different would unfold

The rays began to grow dimmer
And my path would lose its glow
Unfamiliar and distant horrors in the distance
Retreating through the only path I know

Moon beams often allure me
Stars speak of secrets in the sky
The wind however reminds me
How lost one gets in the darkest night

Returning as always to the glowing sun
Perilous and long is my road ahead
Awaiting me is something you've always done
I shall return worn always
Unless I be dead

As the mountains close in on your face
Starring out as the darkness will rise
I fulfill my promise of returning to the place
From where light years I travelled into the skies

I'll go to the moon
I'll become a star
Only for a glimpse of you
Who guided me this far

That Night

As the metal notes reverberate
Each pitched higher than the last
Lucid night, dim lights
And the spells were cast

Music seeping into our veins
With carnal needs pulsating
Not long before the fingers
That stroked the chords traced my skin

Lingering kisses tainted with languish
Tongues caressing and crushing
With no time to lose
You slid on me
Entwining your legs with mine
Delicately unwrapping to seek what lay beneath

Tasting flesh, teasing desires
Igniting and smothering the fire
Pinned and bare I lay there
As harmless as I may seem

Waiting to be pleased
Letting out a moan to invite you more
Panting with passion
As I feel you like my own
Your warm breath in deep recesses

Pulling you closer, you slither in me
Pushing harder till you hit the wall
Coaxing me as you shatter the guard
Surge of pain
Ecstasy follows like molten lava

Hard it is to let go of you
Lying sated
Leaving pleasures at the bay
I snuggle next to you
As tonight I know you will stay

Thorn With Petals

Had to rub my eyes twice
Before I touched this feral thing
It packs a punch of nothing but spice
And its roots, the beauty they bring

Shiny and smooth, I wanted to touch
The mouth however, was too much
Sharp, it cut like my machete blade
The sight I could enjoy, the plucking it forbade

With every effort to feel
The one thorn, my tries it fell
Upon my fingers, the pain was real
It was protective of its assets, I could tell

So I dug into the ground
Yanked the roots real quick
Sting me it did, then lay without a sound
The cure however was in its petal I found

I fell in love, it made me sick
Thorny flowers are the hardest pick

What Shines For Me

Given a bowl of diamonds
Told to pick just one
I'd hunt for days and nights
To find the dullest one

Dull, like a sunset sky
Or a street lights glow
Like the last ray that passes
Through my window

I'd hold it and cherish it
And will always wonder
Why it's so special
To me down under

Is it because unlike the rest
It chose to be sleeping and dark?
Or because it just didn't care
Whether it looked plain or stark?

I chose it because while the others chose to shine
This diamond chose to be itself
And that's perfectly fine
The rarest doesn't want to be the best all the time

Not Thinking Of You

There are these times
When the sun blinds
What I'm looking for
And the wind blows away
The thoughts I want to devote
To the images
Blocked by the sun

Your images
Your lingering gestures
Your melodic babble
Becomes a part of my own voice
These distractions
These inconsiderate responsibilities
Adding to A.D.D.

Never leave me alone with you
Never leave me to stare long enough.
Never let me form a complete picture
One that resides in my thoughts when I'm not thinking
One that occupies my sight when I'm blind
A moment which freezes time
So I can melt at that perfect image

What Nature Can't Provide

The cold breeze still kisses me
And begs me to stay and embrace it
With arms wide open
While the mountain implores me
To impregnate it with my footsteps
For the lonely rock has no kin

Disturbed waters force reflections into
The deepest crevices of my calm clear mind
Nowhere amongst the seductions of nature
Am I content, for they are not my kind

Glistening dew drops smoothen my tread
Urging me to be lost in the jungle woodland
While the stones on which I slowly step
Lead me to a burial ground of sand

This tomb of flesh and blood, desires another
Not made of wet grass and mud
Haunted knowing that nature could keep me still
Lifeless and forgotten against my will

Enticed by the smell of the flowers and the soil
That harbor the caterpillars and worms
The blanket of clouds above and sometimes below
Barely include nature's giving terms

She provides waterfalls, and mountain peaks
Brooks, flowing streams and rocky creeks
Sounds of crickets, silence and more
Hoots of owls which one can never ignore

Howls of mountain dogs, and the calls of birds
Leaves rustling while they're trampled by herds
Fragrances of musk, mint and coriander
Petals colored blood red and soothing lavender

Even so, she can never be true
She'll always be cold, and will be kept apart
Never can she silently whisper like you
Her I love yous, don't come from a heart

Do you hear that? O! Mother of mothers!
That's the sound of a beating heart
Can you ever be so natural like others
And truly love me from the start?

Just As Nature Ever Thought

I see green rocks and green mountains
Blue skies and Blue Mountains
The rush of the Parvati flow
The grey mist I blow
But there's no Butterfly

There's butter in my food
There are flies in my food
Natural grown vegetables tasting
That I can't fathom wasting
I could but it would sadden my Butterfly

My feet forever tapping
My ears are always tapping
To sounds I don't normally hear
It's just something that's not familiar
When I'm not around my Butterfly

Eyes, they see the blue and green
The tongue tastes the natural green
My ears hear only the mighty green
Just as nature enviously thought
With my Butterfly, I was not

Love You Till The End

Walking along the fateful solitary road that night made me realise, it doesn't matter where you begin your journey; what matters is where it takes you. That night, with only my silence and the shadow of death following me, it struck me that this life is too short. If you don't make, it will not spare you when the hungry claws of death come to seize.

Love, a beautiful word; not many don't really understand; until they lose the one they truly love. You fight, you shout, you crib, you cry with that person, but only when you know, that there is no more looking forward to all that, do you understand how many times you sulked and stayed away from the one you loved. You could have sorted it all out with a hug, and lived a happy memory.

That night just etched a horrifying imprint of all my ignorance towards the one I loved, towards all those times when I was busy doing what I felt was more important to me. I now wish I had spent that time thinking about giving it a second chance. Even a break- up or a divorce can be mended but how can you resurrect someone who is no more? What I would give to get another chance to say I love you. Suddenly it was all so dark, I seemed so lost and all I could hear was my heart beat; my only companion for the years to come.

***

I woke up to find myself bundled among the various

equipment of the hospital, the hustle bustle of the patients, the cries of all the new born and the ones in pain. I saw no familiar faces around me, just a nurse who came to me with medicines and food, of which I liked neither. I felt my life was shattered into a hundred tiny pieces and I had to find a way to put them all together. I needed to go back to where it all started.

I am Erik, simple guy living in Burul, a small town near Kolkata on the banks of the river Hooghly. I had left my homeland a long time ago for the sake of my love who lived here in this town. I came to India with her after my post-graduation as we completed together in Berlin. As I followed her here, I began to miss Burnswick. I had given up on my home, my family and everything else just to be close to my love, Rebecca.

She feared her parents would get her married off to an Indian as soon as she got back. I lived in the hazy comfort of being around her for the time being. Rebecca saw how much I had put on the line for love. The fact that I had never spoken to her about it, came to her as a surprise.

***

I still remember vividly the first day I set my eyes on her in college, back at Berlin. I had never seen any eyes so bright and intelligent. They almost seemed to glow with an aura of their own. The light that radiated off her skin seemed to come from within. Her body held the promise of fulfilling any man's darkest fantasies. As time passed we bonded in a friendship and spent a lot of time together. Her independent being and that pious soul attracted me to her like no other women could. Despite knowing her for a year, I was hesitant to tell her how much I loved her, afraid it might change our relationship forever. I knew she trusted me; she ran to me for comfort and to share her joys and sorrows. As time flew, and soon we were at our graduation dinner, clicking class photographs to keep those moments frozen in time.

After that, she took a flight to India and I followed her. I put up in a hotel and then my journey for love began.

A few months later, she learnt I had found work and was well placed in a company. Something struck her curiosity and she questioned me,
"Have you come all the way just to stay close to me?"

Finally, in one fleeting movement, the dam of my feelings that had held up for all those years broke, and the feelings gushed out of my heart to reach hers, hoping that there existed some feeling in her heart too, which would envelope mine and give me a place to settle in.

It began to rain and she walked off without a word. Like a stone statue I stood there for a few moments, wondering why I had gambled away such an important part of my life. I spent the night in great anxiety, unable to sleep or dream. However, the day that followed was highlighted with the bright golden rays of the sun. It just raised my hopes to see the sun appear from behind the dark clouds.

My phone rang and I was surprised to hear her voice. She invited me home for the first time to meet her family. It lifted my hopes further. Later that day, I found myself facing her family, while she stood there trying to explain her love for me, it was a big step in her traditional home, but her parents agreed, without any protest.

Soon, the cog wheels of an Indian wedding were set in action and two souls were happily united.

It had only been a year since we were married and settled in the old city of Howrah. There was growing tension between us. A gradual increase in the number of fights, taunts and tantrums followed for days initially and then, for weeks. I felt the girl I once loved was lost; she ceased to exist and my love grew cold. We got bored of each other and barely spoke, unless we had the utmost need to. We tried to resurrect the relationship we shared in Berlin, but I sadly began to see our love story coming to an end.

With time, the distance between us began to grow vast and we didn't know when it all snapped or we thought it had snapped.

Until that dreadful night…

We decided to take a trip together, to allow dormant seeds of romance to spring back to life. We got onto the high way and somewhere down the road, in the middle of nowhere; we started arguing. Out of sheer frustration I stopped the car in the middle of the high way, looked at her and asked her why we couldn't agree for once. How that love that was once so plush, had withered so easily? I begged her to tell me where I had gone wrong. She had no answer. We sat there in a cold moment of silence in the still car. Without our headlight's being on, there was no sign of our car's existence on the highway.

Rebecca opened the door and got out. Suddenly, a bright yellow beam of light washed us from the rear. Within a fraction of a second, I saw a monstrous truck swipe the passenger side of the car. As its huge tyres rolled right past me, I got a glimpse of Rebecca being crushed to death. Paralysed with shock, I saw myself covered in blood splattered glass splinters.

The truck driver's face was drawn with fear at what he had done. He reeked of alcohol and the foul stench pardoned him from having to explain anything at all. He muttered an aplogy and fled the scene, never to be found again. With trembling fingers, I pulled out my phone and called an ambulance. I struggled and got out and started walking aimlessly on that desolated road. I knew no direction I took would lead to solace, for the only smile I looked forward to, was lost forever in a pile of crushed bones.

***

After weeks of recovery and investigation, I was left to start afresh, but this time without her. I had no hope or reason to live. The detectives handed me Rebecca's phone, as I got discharged from the hospital, for it was the only item of hers they could save from the accident. Whether or not they found the cowardly truck driver, meant little to me, as I would never be able to look into the face of the man who took my Rebecca away from me. Her family was shattered far worse than I was.

I went back to our home, where each corner reminded me of all the happy times we had spent there, and how I regretted all the times we fought, while we could have made love instead. I never knew I would miss her so much until that day. I realized even with all those fights she was still there with me. How stupid could I have been to think that the love existed no more.

One fine day, years later, I came across her phone, her last bit of memory. I had never thought of going through it or reading her last messages. That day, I sat on the edge of the bed and flipped through the phone's contents. It seemed like her physical being was encapsulated in that cell phone. The long list of contacts and names of all the people she loved, her friends and family.

Just, when I seemed to have lived through her virtual being, a message caught my eyes; it read:

I love you and always will for as long as I live, even if we have to stay apart forever."

A pain shot through my heart, when I saw that who it was addressed to; her business client, a man of whom she had spoken very fondly, whose success stories she had often narrated.

It was unbearable, for I knew not who to blame, Rebecca or myself. I will never know the answer, for sure, but the stab of betrayal left a deep gash.

Yet, as I flung the phone out the open window, I closed

my eyes and struggled in agony to find traces of love I had for her.

I felt its presence intact and stronger than ever. Maybe, it was because I knew I could no longer argue with her, or that I was blessed to have spent at least some part of my life with her. Despite everything, I just refused to ever stop loving Rebecca.

Climbing A Ladder

Standing close to a leaning ladder
Path to climb the roof above all
Not for self murder
But an ambition to stand too tall

Broken was the first step
Can't find a way to go further
To the least I may trip
But never choose the latter

I can mend it
Not sure if it will hold
I seem to be throwing a fit
Yet to me I seem bold

To climb, a risk I would take
Failure is acceptable
But can't stand to be proven fake
Every word spoken to you seems like a fable

Though, you need to know
Roof is the canvass of love you spread above me
And my ambition
To have you as mine

The Last Petal

Like the lavender wind
Blowing from the trees down south
You choose to whisper into my ears
Those words of courage

You landed on my shoulder
And I kept you, like I would
Keep a lucky charm, one
Which I cannot imagine myself without

Whilst you lay there
I felt your tenderness show
You presence scented my troubles
And blew them towards the sun

All I have now is this one fragrant possession
That whispers love into my depression
Your petal
Has left an unearthly impression

Hollow Promises

Despite the cold, a soul sold
Fear of desolation
Muted as cries of desperation
Reaching out to its human counterpart
None to care once you depart
Falling tears go unnoticed
For they belong to the diminished

Ears hear the earthly noises
Who recognizes the sound of a shattering heart?
With solitude as it's only companion
For love of thee was so shallow
Hollow promises may not last a lifetime
Pain they cause can survive even death

Linger On

As the night gets colder
And my breathing turns deeper
There is just one solemn desire in my heart
To be calmed by your silence
And to become lifeless with your touch

That my existence be interspersed
With flashbacks of your memory
With reminders you would leave on the surface
In time, they will possess me
Keeping me sane, in a fragranced jungle

So that I may overcome
And become one with the spirit in you
For its nature, forever lingering
Calming the storm, long before the silence
Keeping my heart beating, as it turns cold again

Imagine You There

Sitting under a rock
Watching the clouds burst forth with rain
The ultimate shock
Of wondering if I'll go insane

Haven't eaten for days
Or moved for hours, I dare
Amongst all the chaos, I
Imagine you there

Whispering through the mist
Guiding the droplets astray
Telling me to hold on
Things will soon be okay

And all I do is hope
When I'm stronger I look up and pray
To the rock above to shelter me
Forever from days like today

I don't know how much
More I can handle
It's not long before, I cease to care
Like the last glow of a burning candle, I
Imagine you sitting right there

Flames

Tongues of flames reach out
Not hard to find the spot
In darkness hovers the smoke above me
From smoke you can follow the fire

Choked and smeared by flying ash
For what burnt was only trash
Peace surrounds the crackles
Nothing but a heap left behind

All hopes charred to death
What remains, a mere myth
Did it even exist for real?
I doubt, not me and you, but the deal

Today, you cast a charm
Tomorrow, you shall eat me from inside

Forsaken

Only my echo resonates in the dome
This world has become my sarcophagus
I was a shadow of a being once
Yet I don't even see the silhouette now
What I was and what has become of me
I existed as a being
Not even a mere soul anymore
Wounds bleed, but no one to bandage them
I searched for a shoulder to cry on
But it is lost in the crowd
The sun, the moon
Even they don't matter anymore
You were my days and you are my nights
Moments I spent with you
Race through my mind
Like a spool of a film plays in rewind
The images move so fast, I wondered
If you ever gave a thought to our past
You have tethered me to a forsaken land
Soon, a huge tide will take me with the sand
I will always be fervent
For me it was the love that meant
But now you are gone
And sooner I shall be bygone

Silent Sword

You try to make me smile
When the world doesn't mean a thing
So why would I try, to make you cry
What are you insinuating?

I listen so closely to you
Even though it's through a phone
And your words they stick like glue
But your silence has this tone

It cuts me through
It carves me up
Like a silent sword
My ears are bleeding
On what their feeding
Your silence was the last word

It pierces my heart
It twists in my soul
Like a silent sword
My ears bleed
On the silence you feed me
When goodbye's the last word

It's all over now
You're no longer there
But the phones still stuck to my ear
I whisper 'goodnight'

But something's not right
This silent sword in my head is all I hear

You tried to make me smile
When the world didn't mean a thing
I'm suffering after what you tried
Bleeding to the silence I'm listening

A Phase

Even in the deep slumbering silence
I can hear you breathing
Not something that happens by chance
To know you are close is a feeling
So exhilarating

Teasing me
By your mere aura of presence
If I search
I will find nothing
Though in my heart boils
The cauldron of vengeance
Rinsing my soul of all the cringing

A mistake made
Know not whom to blame
Fate united us
With choice we departed
Our love was real
Not some fascinating game
I try to play forward
What would have happened
Had we not parted

Could I still lie in your arms
Forgetting all the pain in the world
Staring into your eyes
Feeling the pulsating charm

Even in the cold winter breeze
Not feeling the cold
And being with you till we grow old?

Despite all the longing
To be back where I belong
I don't see a reason why I should go back
Where pain will envelope me
This phase is just a change of season
Today, I shed a tear
Tomorrow I will want to break free again, I fear

Pain

I bled in pain
I cried in vain
Some tears I shed
Who knew what had led
Solitude envelopes me
Visions of the past is all I see
After all it was fates call
Darkness so impenetrable
I knew not where I did fall
In the flames of sorrow
I am engulfed
Only to rise as smoke
I left my form behind
May be I was rude
But you were never unkind
With my heart ripped
My soul tricked
Burnt out is the candle of trust
Digressed to lust
And now I so despise
The illusion of love
You showed me
Right through your eyes

The Mask I Wore

After playing with fire
The mask I wore melted to become me
Concealing my face without a trace
Never realizing what was done
A stranger to my own eyes
The innumerable lies I so despise
A boat for those stranded on an island
A threshold for the same
Taking the form of any mould

A piece of clay by nature
And a disgrace to my nurture
Life, a game I played
I won in the end
But lost my soul
All that is left
The stench of the charred flesh
Beneath this mask
No face left to bask
No heart shall ever find
This hollow carcass

Forbidden Fruit

A friendship, at first
Taste matured with time
Playful overtures of thirst
Led to Eve's lusty crime

A feeling, so fine
Just worth the taste
Reaching out to the vine
Efforts not worth a waste

A partnership, then
Bonded by a consented duty
A required time we'd spend
The produce looked more fruity

A sensation, everlasting luck
Pondering where my finger
Should dare to go and pluck
So that the emotion would linger

A relationship, perhaps
Things seem like they could go right
But boldly face the mishaps
Once you've taken that first bite

Betrayal

Faith can tarnish like silver
When it comes in contact with betrayal
Trust can be lost like needle in a haystack
When carelessly tossed

Loyalty can be buried
Like a dead seed in soil
What remains is the impalpable truth
Too good to be a lie

Bonds with traits like these
Only seem to last long
With the pain they leave
Harsh and cruel
Once factual, now become fictional

Neither do they grow
Nor do they die
Remain stagnant
Yet always survive

Severed are the roots of understanding
Nipped are the buds blooming
Only the barks remain
To be weathered with time

Was it worth that alongside we came?
Cherishing a bond with joy

When you knew all along it was just a ploy
A mask on the delicate joint

A tempest of emotion builds
To engulf all the sanity that persisted
Even curses seem hollow now
Only a jinx of destiny can make you bow

Notorious Candle

What is a candle without a wick?
That melts into a blob, without being a light stick
Mold and recast, shaped again with time
Yet sold again without a wick, for a dime
Endless homes it changed
Endless hands that reached out to it, called it damned
In places, it stood staring in vain
And some tossed it away
Like a manufacturing bane
Along came the one who baked it with a wick
Turning it into a beacon of light
It burnt and burnt till it burnt out
Its joys knew no bound
Once it left the maker
Alone it wandered into strange hands
With false freedom, mischief serenaded
Through the flickering eyes of flame
Tantalizing those around
To turn to darkness
So, it could entice them like a geisha
Playing with the wind
All the pawns of the game
Advancing step by step
Shrouding it with their own need
Aroused by the candle's deeds
Burns out the candle sooner that it thought
Molten and dejected
A scrap on the table

None would recast it again
For the dirt it had gathered
Now, time stood still and it wondered
What a candle it would be
Had it remained loyal to its maker?

Quest For Lust

Perfidious half of me
And, there was a she
Eyes that stare
With enigma in them ablaze

Even in the hazel light
The sheen of her skin, a taunt
Her fullness
Pressing against the skimpy dress

A delicate stride
Inviting me, to follow her lead, I abide
Guiding my fingers
Beneath the silken straps

Caressing the soft orbs
Filling my palms with ecstasy
Unleashing my manhood
With a mechanical urgency

Droplets from the shower above
Enamouring, like revealing a treasure trove
Thrust against the wall
Lips locked, tongues laced

Gathering wetness between her legs
The hollow with the hardened tip
Beckoning me

Not now, not so easy
I force her, to beg on her knees
Hands behind her head
Pushing deeper with each stroke

With a jolt, I threw her on the floor
On top I ride
With a rhythm of my desires
Moans that follow, inspire

Sated, I left her depleted
Traversing those familiar roads thinking
With my love at home
I paid for lust
Digressed like some
Only, if she understood
Her curse was my unfulfilled thirst

Last Letter

Melancholy tolls of the bell
From the tower outside
I sit by the window sill, calm and still
They mark the end
But for some they mark the beginning
Cold and dark, it may be
With mists of fog settling

I stare out
Even the neon, not shining so bright
To penetrate this night
I wait in vain
A longing in my heart to abstain
Tears in my eyes are avid
But I see visions so vivid

I thought I could decipher his silhouette alone
Little did I know I would be deceived
I saw the tall figure walking
I knew for sure, it was him
I rushed to the door
To welcome the one, I so adore

He must be cold I thought
Maybe we could share a blanket
An afterthought
I stood there on the threshold
But who walked to me
Was not someone I knew

A stranger to my eyes
Handing me a letter
Without a word
He was engulfed
By the fog again
I read the letter
It just said

One day I would be no more
But don't forget I love you even more
Sorry, I could not cheat death
Only because I cheated on you

Tears and more tears trickle down
I know not, what I lost
Lover who betrayed
Or, a betrayer I loved

Despair In Death Too

Setting sun upon the waves of the ocean
Stars embellished in the sky
Silhouette of the palm playing with the wind
Twigs creek under my feet
Reminding me of my solitary being
As if, I had forgotten my own presence
A distant hoot of the owl
Sound of the lashing tides against the shore
I knew, I was away from the crowd
Concealing myself under the night's shroud
Not knowing
How a tide would sweep me away
And take me to a land
Where I would forever stay
Not another dawn or dusk for me
Not a blessing, my soul heard as I passed away
None to seek my shell that drifts in the bay
You always said
My absence would leave a dent
You would be shattered beyond repair
Follow me now, to where I went
I am no more
Yet I search for your love
And I am only embraced with despair

Last Nail in the Coffin

Ashes of memories fly around
Requiem still resonates in the heart-beat
Smell of death taints my breath
And all I see is the burning pyre

Days ago I saw the light
But draped in darkness now forever
Who knew what the twisted fate had in mind
Even with my sight, it makes me seem so blind

Ravaging flames, eat me from within
My desperate cries to hold you back
Lost in the wisps of wind
Tortured brutally my soul exists no more

Why spare my life
When my life without you is such a strife

Dream

Solitarily, I walked a lonely road
To search for my final abode
Trotting further I saw him waiting for me
Lost in thought under a yew tree

I wondered how he could be such a sage
Even when he knew we were on the last page
We were standing in the middle of a crossroad
That marked the end

Loss and grief seemed inevitable
Though, I knew I had to remain strong
We knew the moments would last till eternity
But, we could not continue our journey

Thrust back into reality
I found him by my side
But I wondered what would happen if that dream came true
I would lose my life's only hue

I realized there is no time to stand and stare
Or dream and share
I washed away the dream with a tear
Though in my heart, it had left a fear

Melting Desires

When the waves of passion cannot be contained
They lash against the ridge
Slip like a tiny waterfall into the valley
The wrath of the tongues is unleashed
Tasting, every fold, every crease

Rhythm of the hot breath against the bare breast
Makes the heart underneath skip a beat
Fingers thrive to trace those smooth curves
With strokes and spurs

From nipples to thighs
And with each slips a moan
Oh! what a tease and then a sigh
Volcano of ecstasy building up

Pulsating and pleading
Touch at the tip, the thrust and the push
Slow and fast
Turning every pain to pleasure

For how long shall it last?
Soon the molten desires flow past

Dragon And The Butterfly

The shimmer in your eyes
When you stopped and winked
Is too distant a sight for me
When I flap my wings, it uproots me
And its impact lasts eternally
When you pollinate, and give life to others
They get trampled when I stroll
My progeny, you see, is just like me
And he doesn't know he has a soul
But never have I seen, such a tender sweet creature
The thought curiously makes me think
Why when you flap your wings
A flame in my heart sings
The impact makes me stop and wink
All I'm made of is tough beast hide
Which arrows dare not penetrate
Castle fell, no survivor tales to tell
And you're given attention in a such a weak state
I can melt boulders with my furious flame
How do you do the same to my heart?
When it is covered with layers
And survived so many slayers
These things have puzzled me from the start
Hear me butterfly, let me fly to the moon
It is you I have to truly impress
There we can be alone
We'll learn everything on our own
In a land which is no more, no less

Uncanny Connections

Connections in the darkness
Respite to have found an old acquaintance
In the plight of the game
Among the chaos of the same
Turning the table of fate
Not realizing it was a bait
Whose eyes gleamed with dreams azure
Words weighed with precision
Every move made with a sense of direction.
Porous sponge of knowledge
Yet living with a fear of the edge
Patience a virtue
An art acquired by few
With a touch of temptation
And skin that reeks of passion
Arms that could wrap you in solace
Rarity, when looked for in haste
Yet, if perfection was living it is you
If there had to be someone for me, it is you
But who can trust the connections made in darkness
They may last the longest or not at all

I Didn't Know

I didn't know
Those words for her
Would hurt you
They were just words
Once upon a time
I didn't know I was
Preserving the past
As an age old bottle of wine
I didn't know I could
Have been so selfish
Defending the person
And not the cause
I didn't know
The repercussions
The aftermath
For breaking such basic laws
I didn't know it would
Grow into a volcano of hate
Overnight, while I slept so softly
The insecurity inside
To avoid such a fate
For which you were tortured awfully
I didn't know how to apologise then
This is now a new song
I know that I didn't know
I just didn't know I was wrong

Blind Sight

We are all blind
And blatantly refuse to see
Beauty of the simplest kind
Spiritual and heavenly

I wish to see
The colour of flowing laughter
Whether it turns us sad
Or makes a happily ever after

Does the larva know?
It can one day kiss the sky
Spread its wings and soar
Out of a cocoon and fly

I see these gifts
Of nature's endless bounty
And I wish I couldn't
For reasons in endless counting

When ice-cream cones
And monsoon rainbows
Look like a moody starless night
The feeling doesn't frighten
When the grip of your hold tightens
And I feel like a flying kite

My sight has blinded me
My thoughts and actions
Marooning me on an island
Made of negative interactions

Your whispers to me
Will never go un-passed
The touch of your skin
Even when your clothes are cast
The push of your gentleness
And the breath of your life
Even when my sockets are hollow
Tell me I'm alive

When you hold my hand
And your hair hits my chest
You wrap my arms around you
And place them below your breasts
I find myself to be blessed
When my eyes refuse to see
This blind world around us
Trying to find what you see in me

Destined

I sat outside the house, watching the flames engulf it; the fiery tongues seemed to be rising without any stopping. No call for help could be heard over the crackle of the flames; eating the insides of a home and turning it into ashes. With no moon in the sky and the image that was unfolding before my eyes, the night could not get any darker than this. Even the stars that usually seem to be the blessings of the departed, seemed nothing more than the eyes of the devil; twinkling with joy as they looked down upon me.

Glass shatters with a crack, a broken heart shatters with a drop of a tear behind the drapes of silence. Tonight, I realized it is easier to gather the shattered pieces of a broken heart only, when they are not yours. For a person like me who was immune to pain, and accepted sacrifices as the parcel that came with love, I lived bravely on the edge. I wish I had someone with me for just that one more time, to take the courage and push me off this cliff. What I dreamed of as eternity lasted for nothing more than a year of countless breathtaking moments.

Devoid, lost, forsaken and frozen and is what I looked like, when I was found by the firemen, who had put out the fire and were helping me to get into an ambulance. The last place I wanted to be in was under the lights, with all the tubes and needles around me. Surrounded by people dressed in the colour of purity; the only colour considered sacred to honour the dead. They found my ID, because they knew my name, Claire. The name did not matter anymore for my identity was lost, the moment I lost him.

As I was being rushed through the city in the ambulance, with the siren drumming in my ears, I was sucked into the memory of a condition similar to this one. It was one of the happiest moments I could recollect at the time.

***

I saw his face glowing in anticipation, he held my hand; his joy seemed to be at its peak, for he knew, this was that one moment that both of us had waited for. That one time when the universe gives you a signal, that two souls are made for each other. The one time I felt no less than God, for I could create life. With things done meticulously, I heard the first cry, the first of many things that all mothers look forward to.

'Mother', the word weighed more than the heaviest sacrifice; the ultimate epitome of love and forgiveness. He was named Eugene; we had everything planned and just then, as I was about to lose my consciousness, I heard the three most beautiful words spoken in a fashion that could never have been doubted; he whispered in my ears "I Love you".
My memory did not end there; for me it was just a new chapter of my life. But, right now as the ambulance halted, it jolted me back to reality. I knew an investigation would soon put them on my trail and I would be denounced as the culprit. I would not be able to explain to them how

helpless I was. Neither did he give me a chance to explain anything. He flung himself off a cliff and did not even look back; as I stood there, hoping he would listen to me, he had already taken the plunge. He was engulfed by the infinite depth of the valley.

***

The nurses were shouting in frenzy, for they saw the amount of blood I had lost. I had no one to seek aid from; I was the one to be blamed. I was being sucked into my sub-conscious again, my guilty conscious. When I woke up I was in another room of the hospital. I didn't know for how long I had slept, but I seemed to have recovered from my physical misery, that I had inflicted upon myself. The mental torture however, would continue to resonate till I would be lowered into my grave. Each time I tried to close my eyes, the vision was so vivid, so real I felt I transported back in time to that fateful night.

The howling winds carried the scent of change, the thick drops of rain splattering against the window panes, were already begging for mercy, at the hands of the wild thunderstorm. Eugene was crying in the hallway; it was the first time he was experiencing a thunderstorm. Suddenly, with a power cut the nightmare began. I left the stove as I was cooking. I went out to search for a torch, but on the way I picked up the baby. Having found no torch but a candle instead, I now went out to search for a matchbox. Amongst all the chaos, I decided to leave Eugene back in his cradle.

As I left my child and entered the kitchen, I failed to notice the odour of leaking gas, I lit the match and there was a huge ball of fire, which engulfed the surroundings sending me flying across the room. With panic and my survival instincts kicking in, I jumped out of the nearest window, completely forgetting that I had left Eugene inside. I was already too late and the house was in flames. The only thing that stuck me then, was that I was a murderer. I saw a shadow hurrying toward me, it was him. I managed to utter enough words to explain that Eugene was inside. The beams were already collapsing and soon the roof fell in too and Eugene's room was the first that had caught fire, being the nearest to the kitchen. I never saw more pain than what I saw in his eyes that night, having lost our son to my follies.

I did not know how to explain what had occurred. He looked at me with anger and sodden eyes, approached the end of the cliff, upon which our house was still burning, and threw himself upto to God. He did not look back, but that last glance said it all. How could I kill what I had created? I wanted to jump into those flames, but, I felt like a coward. I had lost the only two people I loved the most. I stood there alive and it killed me even more. I tried to make my death even more painful than what my loved ones had to endure. I tried to cut myself with a sharp rock. But I only passed out.
Woken up by the nurse, for it was time for my medicines again. Tears and more tears trickled down my cheeks. No one had heard me speak since I had been in the hospital. I was still in a state of shock. I wish I could have gone back in time and changed it all; but I was too far away.

When the nurse asked me as to how I felt, the only words that escaped my lips were "please, let me die;" for she had been trying to save my life.

The words seemed like a blow to her, but they were the pleas of guilt. How could I explain to her the burden of my sin? I took two innocent lives just to save mine. I tried to explain it to her but, she refused to hear a word and instead, put me to sleep. I knew the guilt would haunt me, the look that said, "How could you forget our son inside?". A baby, a just a few months old who could barely say, " Mamma". I was ready to die twice, if only it would help me save those two lives. They made my world and for me it existed no more.

That night, as I lay there thinking of a way, to meet death, the nurse walked in with a baby in her arms. Without any warning she gave it to me. It was a little baby boy; the nurse then slowly told me the story, of how his mother died due to medical complication and she had lost her husband a month back in a road accident, the baby was orphaned the moment it stepped into this world.

I was ridden with sorrow as I heard her and I was eaten by fear from inside that I might harm the baby.

I asked her to take him away and give him to some family that would love him more, having known my story, she felt that baby would become the reason for me to live and repay my guilt. Eugene was a memory, but the baby made me understand, we were made for each other. We had no one except each other in this world.

The next morning, with the first rays of the sun and fresh hope, I decided to write another chapter of my life. I gave up on the thought of death, because I found a reason to live. I held my child close to my heart; making a promise to never let him out of my sights again. I learnt to see the importance of life from the coffin and the power of another soul that resurrected me.

Dare To Dream

Sodden are the dream unfulfilled
Splinters of shattered dreams
Cause hearts to stream
Hurts those who live in a world of fantasy

Causes pain to the ones in lives' ecstasy
Endless joys come crashing down
Uncountable regrets crop up
Mountains of hurdles block the sunlight

Unhappiness shrouds our sight
Tears of loss bind us
For visions we should not trust
Thrust back in to the reality, we realise

There is no time to stand and stare
or dream and share

Behind The Scene

Some dreams are fantasies unsaid
Some nightmares too real to be denied
Some places you have been to
Yet you will never remember the way
Some pits you fall into
Into some you're pushed

Desires twisted with expectations
Hopes for an ocean in a desert
Seeking the heights
Yet forgetting where the climb started
Living without a destiny defined
Some pain uninvited
Some grief we gladly embrace

Some paths move in circles, yet some end abrupt
Crown of gloom resting on your head
Or joy bestowed as a payment
None may be yours
But carry a burden you wish you could share
Some moments pass in a haze

Brush aside the memories
For there exists none to recollect
Crave for not what you want, but what you can have
Don't love every star, for they turn to diamonds
Haste not! You may not live every tomorrow to see it become

I Can Sir

A tiny flame that lights up the dark
Gives life to a paper stick
Filled with Virginia leaves to the top
Filtered, so that you burn less quick

Crackle and glow all the way to the butt
Can you stop it from reaching your end
Slowly ashing the gray cherry top
You carelessly point it at your friend

Burning away the moments of time
Where the wind fights to save your life
The lighter knows it commits no crime
When you dance on the edge of a knife

Nicotine in my brain, makes the pain go
Places, where my troubles do not know
I can sir, it's possible and I know why
The smoke only made my lungs cry

I hear the whispers
Of the filters in my chest
We'll help you swallow your guilt
But the tar we can't digest

I can sir, if you don't believe me
Then watch the round craters appear
See them defile your holy temple
As the last stages grow near

But if I could sir, I would sir
For now I can only hope, says my gut
That I can sir, not burn out sir
Like the Virginia leaves in my butt

Show Mercy

Winds don't whisper tonight
Nor does it rustle the leaves
It howls with the gust so strong
As if it would never cease

It stood there
A living being once
But now a carcass
Wilting with the weather

A cracked bough
And shriveled skin
Treated as if it committed a zillion sins
But none to show mercy

Let alone, none to pay homage to its grave
Blooming and blossoming
Now shrinking and dying
What once supported life

Now it's own, a strife
Sapped of energy
It took years to grow
Now taking years of pain to die

Stab it and kill it
Don't make it suffer
With the smoke it inhales
The smoke that has made you so pale

Oh Human! it's just a tree
See the stains of your crime
You can't remove all the evidence
You were found guilty and you will pay the fine

Tree Of Zorn

If I had tears, I would shed them
For now, my leaves will do
I must act quickly, for if I delay
My mother will not pull through

Now I know my true enemy
I will strike him down before I fall
Although he will rise as his numbers outnumber
It would be an honour to fight one for all

I will use his weapon against him
And will convince my brothers to do the same
Mankind will know a cruel trick of nature
When Gaia's sons beat them at their own game

No longer will you breathe the life we gave you
Now you will not breathe for good
No birds and animals will ever come near me
For I might wipe them out, just like you would

What have I become trying to hunt you?
Am I my brother's keeper, am I hurting him too
My intentions have become so selfish
Its as if I am you

The sun shines bright
The wind blows still
The waters never dry up
But one day, mother earth will

Singes Of The Sun

Over the horizon, out of Mother Earth's edge
Rays start to heat up, your rusty window ledge
Searing through with lust, revealing all the dust
Rise out of the Oriental East, it must

Setting in the West, after the Earth's deep fried
It's what it does best, and it can't be denied
The ozone defence, is starting to look like a flop
Ravaged by UV vandals, who just won't stop

As Mother Earth's ice, goes on melting away
She'll be crying tears of mud and flood one day
We'll all be washed up, that day I think
Unless we make boats that never sink

The reason we're going to drown, is not the sun
It's because we never listened, and had our fun
And as the years rolled by, the sun grew hotter
Earth's ability to sustain life, just grew shorter

"But we're all going to die, so why bother at all"
It's embarrassing how man, can think so small
Yet we complain, "the sun's driving me insane"
We chop down all the trees, and wish for rain

But it's the sun who's warning us of coming danger
Waiting for us to realize, why the planet grows stranger
When we see plants wilt, and lakes dry up
We tell the scientists to go home, and to just "shut up"

If only we woke up to this horrific reality
Took steps to change this eventuality
Then maybe we'll wake up, staring at the sun someday
Saying, "your burning desire has lead us to life today"

Whispers Of The Wind

I watch you everyday
And every day your thirst grows stronger
How I wish it will fade away
I don't think my mother can take it any longer

It's because of you I'm poisoned
And appear darker from time to time
Have I ever cast aspersions on you?
Do you defame me for a crime?

Day by day you slash and burn
The forest through which I once blew
Now all I see is a desert of tree stumps
And the remains of the grass I once knew

You have no respect for the ground on which you stand
You decorate it with plastics and waste
The day comes when you will roll around in your own filth
On that day, your own medicine you will taste

The day you grab what's dear to you
And flee from tornadoes and twisters
You will feel my pain, and the fury of
My vengeful brothers and sisters

You will then know what it feels like
To lose the home you loved for so long

But I will continue to pleasure and please you
For magnanimous I remain
Committing no wrong

One day, you won't find or feel me
But before leaving, I will say
Stupid human
Your greed has blown you away

Nature's Finale

Hear the wind go by
As the night turns dark today
Watch the clouds fade from gray to black
As they quietly make their way

When the moon rises high in the sky
The stars start to dance and bling
The wind adds rhythm to their song
As they resume their twinkling

Hear the wolves howl and the crickets call
The rain to rain the ground
Tip tap tap tap, the refreshing rain
Adds a beat to the monotonous sound

A man watches on, in his home in the hills
As nature's beat beats on
He finishes his drink and goes off to bed
As he listens to nature's song
Dreams of darkness turning bright
Slowly enter the mind of him
Revealing a peaceful tranquility
That fulfills his every whim

With his eyes shut close, he wishes to see
The world dancing to nature's song
With his eyes wide open, he can only be
The one preventing it all along

No matter how many trees are taken
For whatever reason, it's a crime
The punishment is like a dark morning dew
When nature's song plays the last time

Doom Monsoon

The sight was one to behold
And the images you could not forget
Like a blessing of liquid gold
Plaguing numerous lives wet

One could see the fruit vendor
The water masked his earned sweat
In a blanket of glossy silver armour
Which could easily contain his death

And then the running student
Who had fear flowing from his eyes
Unable to catch the last bus
The waters held him and hid his last cries

I perished inside a rickshaw
While motor cars baptised me with drain
Hypothermia could be in the next splash
The 'kiss of kichad' brought emotional pain

But the last victim I saw was floating
And the blood washed up against the wall
The headless mongrel swam silently
Toward the edge of a muddy waterfall

Her Words

Listen to her, and let the words
That escape her lips, forever echo
For it will repeatedly give
And never take more
Than a smile or frown on your face
Which may quite just be you
Not understanding your place

Listen to her cry, and know
That every tear drop was shed
So that you shed a drop of sweat less
For her blessings and hopes
Are righteous and countless

Listen to her silence
And imbibe the intention of good
That will one day teach you
To better your ways
So that you may encounter
Happier days
Long after the day, that will come
When no longer she responds
to the word Mum

Despicable Vows

It was long ago in the 1800's when I lived with my family in the small district of Talismara. We were the most well read and distinguished family which believed in the old rituals of the society and followed them rigidly. I wondered if that was the reason we were the most distinguished of all.

As for me, I became an orphan at the age of 4, and since then bought up by my grandparents. How I became an orphan is a story that shook the very foundations of my beliefs.

My father was suffering from cancer ever since I was born. He died shortly after I turned 4; there was a shroud of gloomy silence that had befallen the family, that was not the worst I had to face, I couldn't help but watch, my mother burn herself alive on the funeral pyre of my father.

My family believed in the old customs, and sati was one of them. I could never understand what my paternal grandmother told my mother; that made her sit on the burning pyre. Why was I orphaned before my own eyes? One died just to get away from the sufferings and the other was forced to join him. In one instantaneous flash, fire engulfed my family and I could do nothing, but helplessly cry.

This memory left a very sore impact on me. I was always inquisitive to understand why my mother did such a thing. I was just told that when you are married you vow to accompany your mate in afterlife. That is what my mother had done; but I was never satisfied by the answer. The haunting image always crept into my memory. My mother didn't even scream as the flames ate through her flawless skin.

I remember that tranquil face, with a peaceful smile resting on those lips that kissed me every night as I went to bed. Those mellow eyes that only radiated warmth, but now all I could see in them were dancing flames. Each time I had the recollection of that dreadful day, only tears trickled down my cheeks. I missed the warmth of my mother's hand that comforted me when I was in pain. What I missed the most was that I could hardly spend time with my parents. Even when my mother was alive, she was busy tending to my sick father, leaving little or no time for little me.

That was the moment that instilled in me a fear of fire. As a child, I always blamed fire for turning me into an orphan.

I spent endless nights wondering why my mother was not by my side. When she gave birth to me, she loved me so much. Yet she followed my father to his final abode because of the vows she had made.

I belonged to a family which followed the rituals like a lost ship following the North Star to find the shore. We were an educated family, and were completely capable of dismissing these vows which did not make sense. But instead we preferred to be played as puppets in the hands of the society, upholding the dignity of the family, my mother jumped into the pyre. She was not given a choice. She always had to do what her family asked her to do.

I grew up to understand this. Instead of the fire I began to blame our senseless rituals for taking my mother's life.

It was not until I was a teenager that my grandmother told me that practice of sati had been followed for centuries. If you didn't follow them, you do not show respect to the conventions our ancestors had set for the generations to come. She refused to disclose more, as I was still too young to understand the ways of life.

As the years rolled by, I saw the sands of time shrivel my grandparents. I could see the signs of an approaching end in their face. I could not help much, but I hurriedly learnt how to handle the family business, being the only heir of the family. I could never get any formal education as I had to help my old grandfather with the family business.

One eventful morning I faced my worst fears as I woke up. I found out that my grandmother had silently passed away in her sleep. I was glad that she did not suffer, but, I knew what awaited me was more dreadful. The last rites of my grandmother had to be performed by me.

The following afternoon, I dutifully performed the rituals with my grandfather and close family. My grandfather was sobbing unceasingly by my side.

As I set fire to the pyre, I stared into my grandfather's blood shot eyes and asked him the only question on my, "will you not follow your wife till eternity, like you vowed to her?"

I never got the answer to that question, but I realized how partial and despicable the vows of society were. I just prayed that someday, someone would raise a voice against them.

My Birth Was Not A Sin

Since the day I was planted in the womb
To the day I stepped into the world
They realise eventually, I am their baby girl

The male harangue
Resonates in my ears
Even as I take my first breath to cry
And then
I find no arms so strong, that hold me tight
Even if I am wrong sometimes
He is always right

The strength of fatherly love is always hard to decline
I accept then, maybe patriarchy is divine
But then, no touch as soft as she caresses me
No support as firm as I take my first step
A place, a paradise, a solace for me
The arms of my mother, as they be

Slowly, I trod the road
I grow up, as I go even further
I notice the shackles of taunts that follow her
Even in silence
I could hear the roar of my father
Pinning the blame on her
Not giving him a son as his kith and kin
Oh! what a sin
A womb that could better be a tomb instead
He so abhors, sharing his matrimony bed

His belief, my shoulders too weak
To carry the burden of business
I wish he could ask me, I will learn and never make a fuss
The seeds of such cruelty embedded in his heart
Maybe it is society that nurtures it from the start
It all begins with a dream
To digress into a nightmare, as I now see

Our world is a stage, where only the males play
Them demanding their own kind
They are strong, they are free
I wish someone would hear my plea
Support them not
They have only a seed to plant a tree
Not the soil to nurture without me

As the sands of time fly by
I see my parents wearing and waning
My time to seek my home approaches near
Though they hold me dear
As I tie the knot
I will lose them, I fear
Nexus of tradition will encompass me
But I will find a flaw and not let them go
The ones who gave me life
Are above those who support me in my life

My being me
Does not decide to whom I belong
This life is not too long
I will be with everyone I love and care

It is not wise to crib and bear
Not many steps to take, before I fall into my grave
My only wish not to abandon my parents
For it will be unfair

Let me remind all, I was born a gem
I lost my lustre
For the way I was perceived by them

Maiden

Crushed under the hardships of housekeeping
They go about without speaking
The burden of responsibility on their shoulder
Is heavier than the one who can carry a boulder
Silence is the language of their sufferings
That is believed to be non-existing
Male dominance is that stage
Ordering them on how they should turn their life's page
Unable to break free from the crutches of male harangue
The chains of bonding, tighten around their ankles
Forgotten is the clink of the bangles
Or the beauty of the maiden
Silence is what keeps them hidden
A time will come when they will break all rules
Becoming the ones who rule
A time will come, when kings will turn to myth
Queens will ascend to where the kings now sit
A race like this will go on forever
Break free from it now or never

Beggar's Question

Astray I may have seemed
Not lying there by choice
But what was deemed
Forced to pay a price
None asked me
As to what I brought?
Who shall tell them
Instead it is a life sold
But that remains a mere thought
No ears ever lent
Yet the stares follow
I wish through the eyes
The message could be sent
As the voice is lost
In the soul's hollow
This shriveled carcass that I carry
Reasonless, manacles of abhorrence
My unsung tale now makes me weary
For I am shunned by my own kind
Dearth-less and dreary
I spend eons on footpaths
With hopes that someday
Someone will raise a query
My heart has always known
It will not be before
My death's aftermath

Rural Misery

I see her everyday
As I walk back home from work
And sometimes when I'm leaving
Staring out of an open window
Watching the 'New World' pass her by
Wearing the same sari always
As if she had not another
I wonder what she sees?

Her head burdened with troubles, she rests it
Along with everything else on her hands
Hoping to find some comfort in a world
That has forgotten her; but I haven't

I don't even know her name
Or what she does to survive
At times a glimpse of her misery and pain
Flashes in her eyes,
And I turn away
As I cross the road; I have troubles too

The thought of her looking out haunts me always
Never have I stopped to find out the truth
I'm afraid her troubles will begin to trouble me

The other day I saw tear tracks
As if the night refuses to leave her
The sun burns hot outside
But I feel she is lost in a wintry desert

Darkness and cold surrounds her
O! Thank the creator
He has blessed me abundantly
I don't know what I would do
If I was looking out of that window
Like a 'black ocean' drowning me
Over and over; I need to breathe
My family awaits me at home
Tomorrow, I will see her again
And the day after that and the day after that

As if it has become easier for her to frown
Wrinkles run all over her face
I remember hugging my children last night
Praying, they never see such days
Praying, hoping, wishing, everything
Why am I crying?
Could it be she weeps for the same?
Will I one day be standing there?
Will I one day be watched by another?

Rooftops, Lanes and Spirits

It was around the time when I was 6 years old

My parents lived separately, and I would meet them in monthly intervals. Fortunately, they lived two lanes away from each other, so it bothered me little why they were living separately, but I never understood why they would never meet each other. My Father was a cobbler and a sweeper, and I was impressed he found the time to do both the jobs in one day. Amma said that he used the money he got to buy spirits.

"What are spirits?" I asked.
"They are evil monsters and ghosts that live inside bottles", she replied.
"Why does Abba want that?"
"The next time you visit him, be sure to ask him, beta".
"But Amma, what do spirits look like, what do they do?"
"Beta, they cannot be seen. It is called being invisible. They enter inside you and make you behave like you have no control over yourself, you talk without knowing what you mean, you also hurt the people you love sometimes. Never go near spirits beta, they won't leave you".

20 years down the line I realised why she said "they would never leave me". She tried her best not to say "you won't leave them". I'm afraid she was right.
After finishing my lunch of two rotis and yellow dal, I went for a walk outside, and met my friend Ziya. I told her everything.

"No, Javed, you are wrong. I will show you what spirits are", she said.

She held my hand and took me to a place I had never seen in Chandni Chowk. On the way I saw broken houses, torn mattresses, people selling spices and flour, people selling bottles and people running from the police.

"The police, Ziya, they are catching someone, let's follow them".
"No Javed, they will catch you and put you in a dark room, with nothing but a grilled window. Trust me, my Abba one day was caught by the police when he had done nothing wrong. The police said he was selling illegal items, but my Abba was selling only sugarcane. They are bad people. Even they have spirits, I have seen them".
"Spirits?" I said with disbelief.
"They are not nice people, Javed, please let's go".
"Wait Ziya, weren't you showing me what spirits are?"
"Yes, Javed, I will, but from a safe location, why take a risk?"

I believed her because she was a year elder to me and she was going to primary school. As soon as I looked up, I saw that a policeman was approaching us.

"Ziya, run", I said.
"Stop, Stop", the policeman yelled, chasing us down the lane near Asif bhai's chicken shop. We ran into a crowd of people and hid amid them. The policeman was a clever one. He began approaching the crowd, asking them if they had seen two children. As Ziya was about to run, I held her hand and told her to wait.

"He'll catch us, Javed", she cried.
"No, he won't, wait and see", I retorted.

To my good luck, I was right, because I was afraid if we moved from where we were hiding, we would attract attention. Soon after the policeman left on another trail, we started to hear loud splashing noises.

"The spirits are near, one man has had them", said Ziya.
"Who has? The washer man, Arif? I asked.

Ziya grabbed my hand and took me to an abandoned building. It had stairs leading upwards to the roof. I had only heard Arif's name and what he did, from my Abba. He lived closer to him than my Amma.

"Ziya, how do you know that this man has been near spirits?"
"I will show you", she replied.

She climbed over the broken part of the wall once we reached the terrace. I was scared to do so, because we were 14 feet above the ground. I wondered if I would have survived if I fell. I gathered some courage, mostly what was left after escaping the policeman, and followed her beyond the wall.
"See, Javed, isn't it beautiful?" Ziya exclaimed.

From where we were standing, we could see at least a hundred feet ahead of us; broken wires hanging from trees which were bending in all directions; roofs of people's houses; people cycling in the lanes below us. We even saw the policeman who was chasing us; he had caught someone. The man had a beard and a moustache, just like my Father. He was probably even as tall as him, but he was not wearing a shirt.

"Come, Javed, look at what Ramesh is doing", said Ziya.

The sight I saw was a strange one. I saw Ramesh wetting clothes and then hitting them on nearby stones and slabs. He made loud sounds, as the clothes made contact with the stones. Then he would begin pressing the clothes to the slab and scraping them up and down on the stones.

"Why is he doing that to the black kurta?" I asked Ziya. "He has been possessed by the spirits. I saw him buy a big black bottle yesterday. It did not have water in it, because it was brownish-black in colour. After drinking two glasses from it, he could not walk straight. My friend, Salim, told me the spirits had entered him and that they refused to go. So he enters his house and starts assaulting the clothes he has to wash".

I stared with utter amazement at what I was seeing. She was right. Did this mean that Abba also beat his clothes when he bought spirits? I asked myself.
"Come, let's go, it's getting late", Ziya said.

As we were returning, I heard the splashes and the loud sounds of Ramesh hitting his clothes. I was filled with so much excitement; I began to tell my Amma about everything I had seen that day. She began to cry. I told her that I would be visiting Abba next week and she began to cry even more. I ran to her and began wiping her tears as I hugged her.

"No, beta, you will be staying with me for a while now", said Amma.
"Why? Amma", I asked.
"Abba has gone away, beta, he will come back in 2 months time", she replied.
"Why did Abba go without saying bye to me, Amma?"
"Beta, he was taken …………..sleep now, you have a long day ahead of you tomorrow"
"Will masterji teach me about spirits if I ask him, Amma? I queried.

"No, beta, don't ask him anything of that sort. I told you to stay away from spirits", she scolded. "Don't let me ever catch you talking about sprits"

Puzzled, scared and saddened I went to sleep.
The adventure I had experienced, had exhausted me.
I began to dream about Abba.
"Where could he be?"

From Above I See

I blink red, I blink yellow and I blink green
I tell you when to stop, when to go slow
and when to be mean
When lost in traffic, you may seem
I guide you through the road
And we make a great team
If you don't listen to me
I shout, "it is better to be late than never"
I wish no misery to befall upon you
If not for me, how will you cross this busy street?

Learn your lesson in time
It is easy to break a rule
Not difficult to commit a crime
Threads of life hang loosely
When you are released recklessly
Trapped in the race you are
You might not choose to be a part
But escape is far

Pursued by the honks of the followers
Who are looking for nothing
But a way to overtake
Slow and steady, you stand nowhere
Trampled are the skeletons before your eyes
Made to bleed again and again
For some it reflects strength, for some it is strain
But who has the courage to pull them aside
And bury them with the laws that abide?

I see the world from above and afar
You go on without thinking
With rage boiling in your veins
Time seeps like water in an hourglass
No matter how many times you flip
It only takes a second to drip

The paths are laid out carefully
Many roads lead to the same destiny
Choices make all the difference
You take the narrow roads and seek the world with close scrutiny
Or you take the big wide roads
And find yourself a part of a mob

True Hues

Crimson is the colour of war
Scarlet is the colour of the heart
Difficult to believe beyond the realms
They are so similar, yet so polar
Some may accept, some may deny
Fingers will be pointed
A rage would rise
It will be the hearts that bleed
Walls of repulsion would separate them
And as the pendulum swings
These walls will become concrete
Only love for peace can soften these walls
Yet peace is so difficult to be found
It is a cycle that shows
This world has no ends to begin with

Seats

It takes hard work and dedication
Precise timing and patience
Not a reservation or an education
When it comes to exams and stations

Follow the rules, and do not cheat
Lest you want others to take your seat
Take time to understand rather than cram
Wait for the open door of the tram

Let the others in
When you know you can't win
Aligning yourself in the row of victory
Is no sin

It may take one try
It may take two
But at the end of it all
There's a seat waiting for you

Swift like the wind
Past the beautiful flowing hair
For distractions such as these
Only lead to despair

Be blind to the lost child,
Or the traveller who's led astray
There are others who have hearts of gold
Alive in the race today

Grab what is yours
You have earned its sweet tasting juice
Or be trampled
Becoming a tool everyone chooses to use

Be the first at the silver railing
Hold your ground against the leaving rush
Swift like Samurai, once you're past failing
Be the seat-claimer and give your thoughts a flush

I Wished

I wished for a silver sword
I worked towards it without a word
There were thorns in my path
I was ambushed many times

To abandon the path,
Never crossed my mind
As I knew the sword
Was meant to be mine

As I lay my fingers on its cold blade
I could not rejoice
There were many around me
With a sword like mine

I decided to distinguish mine
I sharpened the blade with my passion
Which would not dull
Even with the sands of time

But in my journey I came across a crevice
That held the golden sword
A tantalizing prelude
That very few wished to seek

There were thorns in my path
I was ambushed many times
But to give up
Never crossed my mind

As I lay my hand on it
I stood out
I felt proud
The only question that lingered was

Did I do it for the fame?
Is there an end to this game?

Metro Mania

Amongst starving beasts I am, for now
Who have no civic duty, and how?
Their human nature grown dark and cold
Hungry creatures do sliding doors hold

Eyeing the silver empty spaces
Lack of patience, grades them aces
With no understanding, their souls be sold
Eyeing the emptiness, as it were gold

Enter the underground, packing zone
Assorted meats stacked, bone to bone
Your destination awaits, they're sadly told
Spare your comfort on women and old

These suicidal civilians will squeeze 'n' fold
Accustomed to torture, they fit any mould

King and fool, much alike they behave
Leaving less room for thief and knave
While they turn, they twist, they fight
They push, they rush, trample they might

The earnest man, lost to his own care
Struggles to make his troubles bare
Losing sight of what is chivalrous and right
The warm sun turns into a cold moon at night

The feminine feels the fearsome stare
Of an innocent who might not even care
For inside the eyes of another knight
May lie the visions of an evil spirit

Vicious outbursts rise out of anger's delight
Sparked by claustrophobia and a space so tight
Sometimes they laugh, like husband and wife
Most times they look dead and devoid of life

As I exit this civic warzone
Telling my parents I'm safe, through a phone
Knowing it's a half-truth, one they must believe
This world is far from what one will perceive

Loading...

Good Morning
How may I serve you?
Press 1 to start your daily routine
Press 2 to put the alarm on snooze
You have an appointment at 2
How do you wish to spend the 5 hours till your deadline?
Option 1 Look good and take the metro
Option 2 Call in sick
Option 3 Spend money and leave late
Good choice sir
Here is a list of things you can do for entertainment
Choice 1 Listen to your playlist/podcast
Choice 2 Read your E-paper
Choice 3 Check your E-mail
Good choice sir
Warning! There are a few errors which need to be addressed

Error 1 You are on an empty stomach
Error 2 You are still intoxicated
Error 3 Your balance is low
Error 4 You are low on cash
Do you intend to solve these issues?
That is not advised; do you wish to proceed?
Good choice sir
May you have a wonderful day
Thank you for letting me serve you

Addiction

An addiction today
May turn your life into a play
It may sate your weakness
But it will pollute your very sweetness

May be your ultimate desire
But will eventually lead you to your pyre
It may be demanding
But you may not realise you're wandering

May be seductive
Beware, it is vindictive
It will lull you into a peaceful sleep
Only to be awoken by a nightmarish weep

May make you feel complete and whole
But it will only cripple your very soul
So don't be deceived by what you perceive
As an addiction today, will lead you astray

Fake Reality

A fantasy is a refuge
From the harsh realities one can't refuse
If fantasy is gold
Then reality is only the mould
A fantasy is a common string of imagination
Reality provides us with visions of variation
Fantasy is what lies behind closed eyes
Reality is always the opposite
If fantasy is a drop of water in a desert
Reality believes in leaving it dry
If fantasy is a flash of happiness
Reality is the stab of sadness
If fantasy is to soar high
Reality is buried without a question 'why'
Fantasy is for those who believe
In a reality of their own
Fantasies are not the visions we must trust
For fantasies are fragile
Though born out of the ground of reality fertile
They can stand only the breeze but not the storm

Hillness

Once upon a time
I'd strap on my shoes to trek
And climb those muddy hills
The vacations were fun
Sometimes it rained
Sometimes there was sun
Simple childlike cheap thrills

Distant tiny water falls
We'd find rocky running streams
Splashing cold water all around
Nestle, we would
Finding shady nooks
To the best we could
Careless in an insect breeding ground

The journey is now the worst
Indifferent, I pride my blue slippers
And still scale those giant anthills
It's no longer a pleasure
Insects, the heat
Never ever for leisure
Will I settle for peace that kills

Like a grasshopper in a can
Sent to roll down a mountain side
Turning out my insides, way past enough
Can't deal, can't walk

Can't shuffle, can't fly
Hopeless to even talk
It's still a vacation, but it's been rough

Black And White Autumn

Once there lived a child
In a densely populated wood
Who couldn't see the world
The way other children could
He heard and felt the changes
And voiced his worries to say
To his sole Guardian, on a windy autumn day
Can I go see my best friend Petal today?

Her family is sick and so is she
It doesn't look good, but I'd surely say
Maybe she just needs some sleep
She's been awake ever since April
Her friends are always playing hide and seek
Baark and Twiig somehow always find me
And bend down to grab me, whenever I sneak
Leefy always whispers my location to the others
But I secretly really like her Mom
Please don't tell her brothers

Petal stays beyond the eighth wood shadow
Compared to her cousin who stays nearby
Mommy, why is petal crying these days?
She sings to me, but never tells me why
Yesterday I stood right beside her
And I felt her tears fall on my head
They were dry and I crushed a lot of them
I heard sad crackling, when on them I'd tread

I hugged her but she only sang to me
'April is gone and winter is near'
I have never met or seen winter Mom
Why does it fill me with fear?

I can't seem to find her home these days Mom
The shadows in the wood are liars and incorrect
But somehow you always take me there safely
You show me the way, as I always expect
Let's leave when the suns brighter today Mom
I'm sure my friends' shadows will lead the way
But just in case I fall and lose direction
Guide me, but let me find Petal today

Tears shed by the Guardians' eyes
The little boy could not hear well or see
His blissful innocence, Mommy did disguise
When she honestly lied to him in agony
Don't worry my little child
Your friend will be well, sooner than you know
When spring comes next time
The wood shadows will lead you like before
Grab your guide stick, hold my hand tight
To Petal's house we go

Drops Of Dew

As the moon's rays filter
Through the bare branches of yew
They touch upon the delicate drops of dew
These drops of liquid diamonds
Seem scattered and few
Some remain while the rest
One would guess the wind blew

These simple droplets of water
On the blades of grass
Then enamour millions amass
Yet without the moon light
They remain as drab as the shards of glass
Which may be ignored
And may eventually pass

These droplets trickle away at daylight
This is the irony of its plight
Though born and destroyed by the sunlight
Yet, it is the moon which makes them bright

A Night I Remember

Mom. A word most kids learn to pronounce as a toddler, yet the depth of the relationship between a mother and a child lies in the bond of blood that flows through their veins. Not a day can be spent without her shadow. Some, spoilt by her love and some, deprived of her it. Some unfortunate, like me, lost her as soon as we were born. Before I could even hear her soft voice, before I could lie in her warm embrace without a worry in the world, fate snatched her away from me. The only solace that I live with is the fact that she lies in my heart and she is watching over me from heaven.

***

One night, I sat all by myself on a stone, lashed by the sea during high tide, with a full moon, thinking of a night spent there long ago. A tear trickled down my cheek, a lump formed in my throat as I remembered the most profound memory, etched in my heart. The sea was so calm, the moon was high in the sky and I was lonely. To my good fortune, I was blessed with the sight of a shooting star and immediately wished for company.

A few moments later, I saw a lady walking towards me from the forest that surrounded the beach. The moon bleached her skin and she had the aura of an angel around her. She walked up to me and said,

"Why are you sitting alone on such a beautiful night with sadness portrayed all over your face?"

"I am lonely and I wished for company."
She replied, "You're never alone, child, you just need to listen to the heavenly voices of creation. Heaven listens to us all. "
Yet, in denial I retorted,
"Heaven doesn't listen to me."

She began to explain how she lived in that forest all alone; yet never felt lonely, because she had befriended the children of nature. I questioned her as to how she did that, and then she made me listen to the whistling woods, the hooting of the owl and the rustle of leaves under the body of a snake. She showed me how she spoke to the moon which would shy away and cover itself with dark clouds. As, she walked into the water it rushed forward to touch her feet.

She explained why the woods were happy. There was a breeze, the owl was hooting to tell babies, she had found dinner and the snake was on its way to pounces upon a sleeping rabbit. I slowly began to feel the presence of so many things around me. I felt foolish to seek a human companion, when God had given a voice to every living thing he created. I reflected, 'Loneliness is an enemy for those who do not have the patience to listen to what silence has to say to them'.

It began to dawn on me that I was not really lonely; I had just surrounded myself with a shield to keep myself away from the world. I understood that there is so much happiness in the world; it could last forever, if only it is shared.

"I can't thank you enough; you have opened my eyes to a great deal of joy today."; I said.
"I have just one more thing to show you my child" she replied

She began walking towards the sea, against the backdrop of the rising sun, playing on the crisp morning waves, until only a silhouette was seen.

But then a scene began unfolding before my eyes, which I could not believe. She walked and walked deeper into the beckoning sea and suddenly a high tide engulfed her and she was gone. Was she human? Or divine?

I still don't know. However, the loss I felt was very profound. Through the lesson she taught me, I could still feel her presence in the little things of nature; at dawn I walked back home with a memory. The illusion was vivid. It engraved itself into all my dreams.

Years rolled by and I could never solve the mystery of who that lady was.

Until one day when I stumbled upon my Mother's old diary. It had a stark picture of her in her youth; smiling back at me from a black and white Polaroid. The striking resemblance between her and the lady I saw at sea was unbelievable. It brought back a flood of memories again. The pieces of the puzzle began to fall into place and it all began to make sense. Today I am back again at the very same spot; sitting on a stone, lashed by the sea during high tide, a full moon; amongst friends I never knew I had.

The most pleasant thought of all however, is the belief that the ghost of my mother watches over me.

Playful Times

Cacophony of innocence rings in my ears
What may be noise for some as they hear
Yet, a sweet reminder to me
Of times when I was free
I knew the only worldly pleasure
Was a laughter seizure

Cocooned in the parental love, so pious
Without wings to search for a love
With perceptional bias
With docile ambitions
Untampered by the rat-race missions

Truth in every word spoken
Unable to recollect any promises broken
Peace flowing in my veins
Not hassled by guilty chains
Such were the times not long ago
But, somewhere I let my values forego

Lunch Box

Press up
Do not use in case of a fire
Three gray walls
No way out, once you're in

I was excited and cautious at the same time
Those doors might squash me
Like bread sandwiches cheese
Dad makes delicious breakfast
3rd floor, 4th floor, <Ting>
Jumped in, feeling the slight tremor
G turned red

I wanted to press the buttons myself
Solo mission
I would tell everyone else later
That I'm a big boy; big mistake

The lights began to flicker
The pulley overhead began to groan
Staring at the ceiling I saw the small fan
Start to spin slower and slower
G would not turn any redder
3rd floor, 2nd floor, 2nd floor, 2nd floor
Tube light please don't go off
I'm scared of the dark
G turned black

I began to look around, three gray walls
No way out, once you're in

Daddy always made a smiley with ketchup on the cheese
I sometimes like to have an open sandwich
But no matter how hard I tried, it did not open

I sat cross-legged on the floor
Pretended that I could open the door using my Jedi mind powers
The harder I concentrated, the more I worried
My sweat began to mix with my tears
And there flowed a stream of sorrow
My heart began to race like never before

I'm sorry mommy, please take me home
Daddy, I'll never ask for anything else again
The louder I screamed
The clearer I heard myself
Hammering on the metal
The vibrations began to echo
I began pounding on the next wall,
And then the next, and then the next

The tube light gave me wink before saying goodnight
My hands turned red, I resorted to open hand
I pulled off my shirt, and aimlessly began to whip the door
With no watch, it felt like forever
The thirst began to dry me up
Lying in a corner, which felt the coldest

I huddled and began to see visions of my past
Alas, my eyes shut close, and all I heard was my mother screaming
Wake up son; mommy's here, she's got you

The lights began flashing by, I was flying
Landed in a soft white cotton bed
It was warm, and once again I shut my eyes
I do recall two men prying the sandwich open

The next morning, I had a glass of milk,
And watched uncomfortably as my dad made himself
A double cheese surprise with ham
A silent wave of horror consumed me
As I watched his palms close

Eternal Hope

Clouded skies beyond the horizon
The night slowly crept from behind
Lost and hungry for survival
Doubt filled the crevices of my mind

Not at all how it was planned
Far from the way, it was supposed to go
A hole beneath me, was dug so deep
Taken to a place, I'll never again know

The last breath in my chest asked me
If I could hold on to it anymore
Life drained dry like a desert of death
That moment was years ago

It was darker than six feet under
Colder than a cannibal's heart
The last breath in my chest saved me
It was determined to do so from the start

Is this all a dream?
A flashback from a life before
Just a new life out of an old life
Start learning there's hope
Burning beyond your core

The first drop of rain touched my lips
Light from heaven helped me to see
Hope defeats all ifs
It's not a miracle how it clung to me

From Wick And Wax

I am spent, hurt and used
But not tortured and abused
For my purpose is complete
As the flames reach my feet

I show you the way
No matter how far you're lost
I'll be your anchor
No matter what the cost
I may die before I bring you to the end
But never forget the light I did lend

The flicker that showed you direction
When blinded was your condition
With only a moments introspection
I can complete my mission

Hold onto the light
Drive the dark out
Hold onto hope tight
Tell the world what it's about

Learn

At the break of the dawn
Just when settled the storm
A phoenix from the flames arose
Every anguish froze
A time of resurrection
A time that only lasts a fraction
Frail and fragile are the threads of life
Just like hot butter on knife

Race against the avalanche
Zenith is the limit
Time is so sparse
From the light of the day till twilight
After all, who can count on the night?
Today you stroll through the blazing inferno
Tomorrow you plunge into the deep sea
That is how you are taught
Life can never be sold or bought
Don't read the map before every turn you take
Learn to put things at stake
What you have today is the neon light
No one knows how long it shall last
Before it will burn away

Lake

In the azure sky, beneath the glowing sun
Lay a silver lake, as shiny as a silver plate
In the wide starry sky, beneath the moon's light
Lay the glistening lake as dark as a black forest cake

Beautiful though it looked, beneath the sun or the moon
Glistened in the morning and shimmered at night
It made the rising and the drowning sun
Dance upon its shimmering tides
Smiling, as it shimmered in its own way
Amidst nature's green, lay the silver lake
So pure and serene

Heavy clouds of rain hovered over the mirror lake
Winds of storms made its silent water ripple with anger
Though the lake was disturbed of its dream
It decided to draw upon its swords and scream
On its way, it splashed the water on the bay
It gulped the rainy water and increased its expanse

Today the lake is a flowing brook
Flowing through every corner and nook
Striding forward to reach its goal
Flowing between the mountains and valleys
Watching its dream come true
To join the sea blue
A chill ran through the brook

And it found itself stagnant in a pit
Only then did the lake realize
It was a dream shattered by the winter chill
That had frozen its waters
And made it a blob of ice

Then understood the lake
It is better to be awake and wise
Than to dream and die

Leap

Sound of the crickets from the window sill
On the foggy night
The croak of the frogs from the pond beside
Mesmerized in thought
My life seems such a mess, I wish to sort

At the feet of Olympus, I beg to know my fate
What good are those sounds which seem like noise?
I shall not call it my attitude, but my poise

I knew not my folly
But it was my ignorance actually
For God does not play a trumpet to pronounce your destiny
For he wishes you to read the signs instead

As the crickets and the frogs say
"Don't miss a step
Look before you leap
Owing to a fear
Of what lies ahead
May be deep"

Beam

As I sailed away from the shore
I could see the beam of the lighthouse
Sailing away from it
Closer I felt to the light
But was only an illusion
It surveyed the ocean with a keen eye
Sparkled me with light
And made me shy
But as it surpassed me
It dowsed me in darkness
I wish I could hold on to it
Though I knew without it
The ocean would be a mess
Badly tossed by the waves
Reflected back at it
I saw the beam trace its own path
To help the ones in distress
Its courage never faltered
Its path never dwindled
There was no vengeance in it's strive
All it wanted to do
Was to save those who survive
What an illusion for many
A ray of hope for some

Light Of The Future

In artificial emergency light
Days before my exam
I sat up while my home slumbered
And I studied all I can

The whirring of the conditioners
Slowly came to a still
My father's respiratory motor
Died without electricity's will

The coolness of my room
Became my body heat in time
Sweat began to escape
Like it fled from a crime

Ticking of the clock
With the snoring of the asleep
Made me concentrate on Freud's
Dream Theories so deep

Not knowing when
The lights will return
Leaves me with one choice
To learn and burn

What can one imbibe ?
But the glow of the only light
Shinning with a purpose
Burning with all its might

I spoke in time
The rogue lights returned
Spinning the fans
Reviving the concerned

The air begins to move
And I feel the urge to read
After all, I need to finish
This book before I sleep

But now I see the device
That saw me through the dark
I now see it with a less purpose
The difference is strangely stark

As I reached out
To turn it off, I see
The hope it gave away
In a dark emergency

Last Night's Dream

Behind closed eyelids
I saw a sight to see
Dragons and butterflies
Living in perfect harmony

Angels and demons playing chess
While they sipped on lemonade
Not a drop of blood spilled
After every apparent checkmate

Lions chasing down gazelles
And when the prey was caught
They'd make love under the stars
Law of the Jungle! It was not

Wings grew off wolves and bears
Birds grew gills and could dive
A mysterious land devoid of cares
Even death began to feel alive

Destiny

When life forsakes you
No land seems to be your own
Even the sea lashes high
The tides are born only to drown you

When the sky carries only the sound of thunder
And all you see is the strike of lightening
That's when you know
Fate is written by the unknown
Where denial is not known

Sufferings become the very roots
Sapping every emotion
We question our very existence
'The clear stream of reason loses its way'

Sometimes we realize
It's not about our happiness
That we should care
It's about the sorrows of other's
That we can share

Why I Can't Write?

Why does he write?
There's never a sole reason
But when a writer doesn't write
One can't imagine the trouble he's in

Maybe it brings back bad memories
A devotion poisoned by evil
The pains taken and the results strange
Making desperate calls, he will

Some promised him fame
Some sold him fake appreciation
Most told him he was lame
And warned him of coming depreciation

But why did he go on?
What purpose could he fulfill?
Or what kept him in those dungeons?
Where he would stare out of a window sill

Why could he not hold that pencil?
And confess to poetry his love
Why could he not write to the sky?
And at night the stars above
Why did he not see the butterfly?
That sat by his cell all day
It must have had gardens to visit
But I'm sure it had something to say

Well no matter how much he fell
And no matter how much he did break
Question not this creator's poetry now
The maker is always proud of his make

I Wrote This About My Co-Author

Shreya Sethi:
An exotic combination of independence and emotions neatly wrapped up in a tiffany box, is how I will describe the incredibly adroit wonder-woman. Her mysteriously enchanting words have led me to a number of epiphanies. A poet in the truest sense replete with experiences far beyond the imagination of most. Prides me to say that you will never hear this sort of self- appreciation from her.

Craig Dominic Pinto:
Synonym for literature, art, music and long hair. He dreams big and knows how to give his dreams wings. Fame and fortune don't make it into his definition of success, but family, friends and this book do. He plays with words like puppets on his fingertips yet they fail to mask his true mellow self behind his rustic exterior.

www.ingramcontent.com/pod-product-compliance
Lightning Source LLC
Chambersburg PA
CBHW022116040426
42450CB00006B/730

* 9 7 8 9 3 8 8 9 3 0 6 5 9 *